Georgia WISDOM

Linda Smith Church

ISBN 978-1-0980-7021-2 (paperback)
ISBN 978-1-0980-7022-9 (digital)

Christian Faith Publishing, Inc.
832 Park Avenue
Meadville, PA 16335
www.christianfaithpublishing.com

Printed in the United States of America

To my supportive husband, children, grandchildren, great-granddaughter, and to my mother, who taught me the love of reading and writing

A WALK AMONG
THE DEAD

There is nothing prettier than Savannah, Georgia's Bonaventure Cemetery in spring. The lovely azaleas are blooming and, along with the flowers planted by family members, the colors brighten what could be a dark and forlorn place. We have been there before. We have read the accounts of the ghosts who live there among the flowers and trees. Kathy, my daughter Shann, and I have come to walk among the dead.

We have seen the sweet grave of little Gracie with its fenced life-size monument of this little girl. We have read her story. It was a sad story, and it could easily bring tears to one's eyes. One so little, taken so soon.

We had walked among the Jewish graves with the tiny stones that rested upon the headstones of the vast number of graves. We left stones as a reminder that a living soul had visited. I am touched by the knowledge that I have a Jewish heritage and wondered if any of them were my family. It was a thought-provoking and heartfelt feeling to be present at these acres of Jewish remains.

We looked for it, but we could not find the little grave of two babies who were huddled in each other's arms, buried together under a monument, depicting how they would comfort each other through eternity. This must have given comfort to a grieving mother and father.

Our trip to the main office produced a map but to no avail. We could not find that little grave. Our memories failed us. We rode over the cemetery. We walked. It began to sprinkle rain. Already three funerals had arrived, but we had yet to see the new graves.

The cemetery is enormous. We rode some more. We walked some more. We were determined to find this grave.

As we spread out among the graves, a young woman was walking toward the cemetery office. I offered her a ride, but she refused and continued on her way. Kathy and Shann were visibly upset.

"You don't know her," Kathy said.

Shann followed with, "Mother! You are going to get yourself killed! You taught me to never pick up a stranger, and here you are, offering one a ride."

"Y'all are with me. I don't think she looks like a killer. And we are just going to the office," I stuttered, knowing they were both right.

I know that God has put me in a small town so I would know everyone. We argued even though I know they are right. Never pick up strangers; never ever pick up strangers, especially in a cemetery.

I turned to look toward the young woman. She was gone. I could see the office from where we parked, but she was gone. How fast was she walking? We each thought as we looked on either side of the dirt road that traversed the Bonaventure Cemetery. She had simply vanished in the misty rain.

It's me, Lord, thanking You for the beauty you created in a gray and dismal place like Bonaventure Cemetery.

A little Georgia wisdom: pay attention to your surroundings, listen to your inner voice, and your family's sound advice: don't offer folks you've just met in a cemetery a ride.

8

AN ADVENTURE
WITH THE
KLUTZ SISTERS

A journey with the Klutz Sisters ended with them making their way down a small, quaint lane. It started when the two of them traveled to Townsend, Tennessee.

Kathy and I love to travel, take pictures, and meet new and interesting folks. Kathy loves to travel to exotic places like Egypt, Israel, Nicaragua, Uganda, Peru, Jamaica, and Jordan. Me? I've been to Canada, Mexico, and Germany with a car trip from there to Belgium and Switzerland with a stop at one of the London airports, and a cruise took me to islands in Caribbean. One of the many reasons I haven't been to other exotic places overseas is that I don't like to fly over water. Now, to many of you, that seems foolish; but to me, it is a big deal. But again, I have wondered away from the topic at hand.

We were in Townsend, Tennessee, and we were having such a quiet and pleasant visit. It truly is the quiet side of the Smokies. We hadn't even turned the television on in our room because we loved the sound of silence. Kathy read while I wrote.

Today we decided to ride up to the Great Smoky Mountain Heritage Center. I was following the signs, and when it said turn, well, I turned. I ended up on this quaint little narrow road, which I was soon to discover was a bike trail. Yes, you read that right! I was driving my car on the bike trail. I was trying to get off as soon as I possibly could, but you know how it is when you are trying to hurry: time slows down.

Did anyone see us? Would they recognize the silver car with the great big red *L* on the tag on the front and the two grandmothers in the car? Would they know it was us when they see us in the local restaurant? Embarrassed, I pretended to know what I was doing. Driving that car on the bike trail pictured here with my chin up and my eyes on the road/trail as if I knew exactly what I was doing. I think the fact that Kathy was laughing hysterically might have given the hint we were in the wrong place.

Later, Kathy and I were in the Carriage House eating our dinner when we realized the Klutz Sisters were now using a car as their mode for klutziness!

The Klutz Sisters visited Biltmore house in Asheville, North Carolina. There was snow on the ground. So what did the Klutz Sisters do? Instead of riding the nice safe shuttle from the parking lot to the Biltmore house, we decided to walk. Yes! Walk! The two women who can't stand on dry ground decided to walk down the hill on the snow-covered trail.

At the halfway mark on this snow-covered trail, we realized how foolish we were in trying to walk downhill in the snow. Southern snow is different from Northern snow. We have much more moisture in our snow, which causes a lot of ice. So one is really walking on snow and ice.

We were holding on to each other. We were laughing at the thoughts of taking a broken bone home as a souvenir from our trip; we were laughing at our stupidity at our age.

But there is a good ending. We made it to Biltmore house. It was beautiful and worth the walk…in the snow.

We took the shuttle back up to the parking lot to our car. We had learned a valuable lesson: walking in the snow is not as easy as it looks on television, nor is it as easy as we remembered when we were children.

We were having business cards made to identify us as the queens of Klutzville.

I can see the business cards now:

Kathy and Linda Klutz
Queens of Klutzville
Broken bones, twisted ankles, and wrecked cars
Extraordinaire

It is me again, Lord, thanking You for taking care of the Klutz Sisters.

A little Georgia wisdom: When traveling, make sure you know the best ways to travel, by car or by foot. It could take you to exotic places.

ARE YOU IN YOUR MISSION FIELD?

Take a minute and think about this particular stage of your life. Are you doing something you really love to do? Do you look forward to each day? Are you retired? If you are retired, how do you spend your time? You just may be in your mission field.

Years ago, I thought God was calling me to the mission field; however, I was too young to realize that I could ever be a missionary. I certainly was not good enough, and I certainly didn't have the Bible knowledge that a missionary would need. I was female. I had never been away from home. The excuses were always ready whenever the thought of being a missionary would go through my head.

Years passed and the tug at my heart faded. I moved away from God. But God never once left my side.

My life had very strange twists and turns, heartaches (many heartaches), and I made a lot of wrong decisions. I couldn't focus on a future; I lived one day at a time.

One day, I found myself in a position with two small children and a poor economy, which had taken my job. I believe this to be one of the low points of my life. I had two choices: I could feel sorry for myself and blame God for my misfortune, or I could do something constructive about my situation. I chose to stop living without a tomorrow and to begin looking toward the future.

I evaluated my options. I had absolutely no money. I was drawing unemployment, and I was actively looking for a job. I had a lot of time left over in the day. With prayer for strength, I made a tough decision—I would go to school. I would go to Piedmont College! This is where you are shaking your head and thinking I have lost mine. No money and going to school? How do you intend to accomplish this, you are asking yourself, right?

The longest walk was the steps going up to the front door of Daniel Hall at Piedmont College in Demorest, Georgia. I had parked across the street from the school and took the flight of steps. This became symbolic of the road ahead of me. It began with the first step and kept going upward as I worked toward my goal.

The registrar's office was on my left as I came through the front door of Daniel Hall. I went through the door to his secretary and said simply, "I want to go to school, but I have no money. Where is the Financial Aid Office?" Instead of telling me where it was, she took me there.

The gentlemen who worked there were attentive, and I left with a handful of financial aid forms. As the years have passed, my advice to all students has been, "Always complete financial aid forms; you never know for what you might qualify, and all you have invested is the time it takes to complete the application." The time it took to complete each application was a major investment in my future. I qualified for grants! Yes, grants! I didn't have to pay them back! God was moving me closer to a mission field from which I had excused myself over ten years earlier. I did not recognize He was moving me closer to His original plan.

I was able to start Piedmont College the fall of 1975! Education was my goal! I wanted to be a teacher, a fourth-grade teacher. My logic made perfect sense: I was taller than the students, and they could go to the bathroom by themselves.

The road wasn't easy. There were obstacles—lots of obstacles! Keeping a focus on my goal was not easy. God walked with me even when I thought He had forgotten me. God never leaves us; we leave Him.

Graduation from Piedmont College materialized my goal. With the help of my mother, who kept my children so that I never had to worry about them, and the wonderful hand of God, I had reached my goal of a college diploma.

Years later, I realized that God had put me in the middle of a mission field: the classroom. I was teaching. No, not with fourth graders, but I was working with teenagers, and loving every minute of it! Now you are saying, "Whoa! Public school in America is not a mission field!"

A mission field is where God sends you. It is up to you to develop that field. Public school in America is not a traditional mission field, but the American Civil Liberties Union (ACLU) can't regulate your personal spirit: the spirit of your smile, your spirit of compassion, your spirit of giving, your spirit of love for one another; and they certainly cannot regulate the spirit of love the students show toward their teachers. One does not have to quote scripture to show the love of Jesus Christ each day.

Where is your mission field? We greet each day with a mission in life. We were given this mission by Jesus when He said for us to love one another. Are you working in your mission field today?

It is me again, Lord, thanking You for not giving up on me when I was giving You excuses for why I could never be a missionary. You, Lord, knew exactly where I would be and brought me the students who needed me as much as I needed them.

A little Georgia wisdom: If you are not happy where you are in life, maybe you are not following God's plan for you. Take the time to learn what God's plan is for your life. I promise you will enjoy the outcome.

AUNT DOVIE AND GREEN BEANS

O n a summer's evening, when the sun is setting in the west and there is a cool breeze, I think of Dovie. Dovie would bring her grocery store paper bag with her neatly folded night clothes to Mama's. She would walk the short distance from her house to ours. When it rained, my brother Eddie would drive to her house and pick her up. But it didn't matter how she got there; we enjoyed her company.

Many summer evenings, when the green beans had outdone themselves and overflowed the vines, we would sit outside in a circle with a copy of *The Anderson Independent-Mail* newspaper opened in our laps and string and break green beans. In the middle of this circle was a dishpan or a foot tub in which we threw our beans as we broke the small pods. Neighbors came and participated in this activity, and we all caught up with the news of the day. This, my friend, was better than television. Now I'm not saying I loved to string and break beans, but I loved the company. As told to us in 1 Timothy 5:5 (ESV), "She who is truly a widow, left all alone, has set her hope on God and continues in supplications and prayers night and day."

Dovie was a self-proclaimed Poor Ole Widow Woman. Uncle Roy had passed in 1967, and Dovie was left with no children but plenty of nieces and nephews who loved her. She had a younger brother, who visited her often. Dovie was never without help, but I'm sure she missed the closeness she had with her loving husband.

Aunt Dovie lived a long life and was, herself, a wealth of information. She was up at dawn and worked until the late evening. She believed you were to hoe your garden early in the summer mornings before the sun was hot, and that the afternoons were used to get things done around the house. She stayed busy. Early mornings, while the dew was still covering her plants, she was busy hoeing the rows of beans, okra, tomatoes, and corn. She saw the sun rise over the eastern horizon and welcomed the new day. This method really worked because her gardens were always yielding an abundance of produce of which she spent many days filling Mason jars or canning the bounty at the local cannery. She also filled plastic freezer bags to store more food in her freezer. She was like the industrious "ant" preparing for the winter.

Aunt Dovie lived through the Great Depression of the 1930s. It was because of this hardship that she made sure she had plenty of food saved for the winter. She had a storage room, with shelving on three sides, in an outbuilding in which she stored all her canned foods and a freezer on her back porch filled with even more food. She would never go hungry.

She would shake her head at a bag of store-bought potting soil. Aunt Dovie never bought dirt. As a matter of fact, she thought a person was crazy to buy dirt. She would get her bucket and shovel, and to the woods she would go. She would dig away the leaves and look for the blackest dirt she could find. This was the richest dirt to use.

After filling her bucket, she would go to the barn, where she gathered the rich deposits of the cows. Mixing the manure with the dirt, she would plant the young seedlings in pots. Her plants came from folks who let her have cuttings or seeds; her plants were beautiful. Her words of wisdom: "you must ask for cuttings or seeds; if not, the plants you took without permission will die." One should never steal a plant, cuttings, or seeds. Dovie was wise in the ways of gardens, whether it be vegetables or flowers.

Aunt Dovie lived through a time when ladies' dresses touched the ground. She told me how, as a little girl, she loved to watch the long skirts roll the little stones as the ladies walked in their long skirts. That was a good memory of her childhood, which held too many painful ones. She made lye soap, processed home-butchered hogs and beef, worked as a cook in a local elementary school; and she was faithful to her church.

Dovie was the only daughter, and her father had the ultimate say over her decisions without questions. When she was eighteen years old, she eloped with my uncle Roy. They left together in a horse-drawn buggy and went to the church, where they were married. Her father came looking for her with a hickory switch to whip her, but by the time he found her, she was already married to my uncle Roy; therefore, she was spared the rod.

Roy was a bit older than Dovie and had fought in World War I, so I don't think her dad wanted to take on that argument. Roy passed away at the age of seventy-eight years old. Since there were no children, Dovie was alone. She often referred to herself as a Poor Ole Widow Woman. Our family loved her, so we made sure Dovie had whatever she needed.

Before Roy passed away in 1967, he was very sick with diabetes among other illnesses. He lost his ability to drive a car several years before he died. To help, my daddy taught Dovie how to drive. She was fifty-four years old at the time, but necessity is a great motivator. She learned to drive that 1954 pink Plymouth and got her driver's license. She could now drive Roy and herself to the doctors, to town, to church, and herself to work. Later, after Roy passed away, she would drive herself and my young daughter Shann places.

Once, she and Shann were going to town. As they were leaving the house, Dovie locked her back door and then fell. Shann was only four years old, but she managed to use the old-fashioned skeleton key to open the locked door. Her tiny little fingers managed to dial, on a rotary telephone, my dad's seven-digit phone number to get help. Shann calmly told my dad, "Papa, Dovie fell, and I can't get her up." My granddaddy and Daddy responded to the house and helped Dovie up on her feet. This was the beginning of her decline in health, and at the doctor's insistence, relinquishing the keys to her car. She lost her independence.

It is me again, Lord, thanking You for the gift of wise folks like Aunt Dovie.

A little Georgia wisdom reminding you to talk to the elderly in your life and treasure their advice. It never hurts to be prepared for the future.

PEACHES AND
SOAP SUDS

Summers were always filled with adventures. You have read about my cousins and how much fun we had growing up. We were a close family and to some degree, we still are. One of my favorite memories is going to Commerce, Georgia, and spending a week with cousins Carol and Nancy. Carol and I are the same age; Nancy is younger.

They lived in one of the neatest houses. It had bamboo cane growing in the backyard. Great fishing poles came from that cane. Uncle Hollis could take a section of the larger cane and cut it just right, and it became a bank with a slit in the top to put in our pennies, nickels, and dimes.

Their house had a very long screened porch across the front of the house. There were plenty of chairs on which to sit if we ever got still enough to sit in one. A visit to Uncle Hollis and Aunt Julia's was a treat. Carol, Nancy, and I played for hours on end. It was a favorite place to visit and stay overnight. I was staying for the week when the peaches were ready to pick.

Uncle Hollis brought home several bushels of peaches. We were to become the "Peach Machine!" Gathered on the long screened porch, all of us worked with the peaches. We peeled peaches; we cut peaches; we preserved the peaches by putting them in Ball canning jars and freezer bags; Aunt Julia pickled peaches; we had peaches coming out of our ears!

We worked on peaches all that week It may have been only a few days, but it seemed like the whole week was dedicated to peaches. The "Peach Machine" had done its job. We had been instructed and trained by the best: Aunt Julia.

To get to the kitchen we had to go through a large living room and an even larger dining room. Can you imagine the peach juice dripping on the floor as we carried large containers through these two rooms to get to the kitchen? Thank goodness there was no carpet on the wooden floors.

Aunt Julia gave us the job of cleaning up the floors in the two rooms as she finished preserving the peaches. It was a job for the strong and creative, and Carol and I were just the ones to do it. We filled a bucket with warm water and detergent. We started off with a mop and it loaded with the soapy mixture. We didn't squeeze the water out of the mop; we just slapped that wet cotton ball attached to the long end of that stick from the bucket to the floor. The suds were great! We may have used a little too much, but we were on a mission to clean that floor! The "Peach Machine" had become the "Cleaning Machine!"

Aunt Julia strongly suggested we clean up the suds. With the towels she provided, the living room and dining area became a skating rink. We would slip and slide across the floor on the towels. We raced; we fell; we got soaked, but we had so much fun. Nancy was taking her turns, but she was younger and couldn't get the hang of it like we did. We busted our bottoms a few times, but you know, it didn't seem to hurt. When you're having fun, one doesn't feel the pain.

It took longer than it should have to clean up our mess, but Aunt Julia didn't get upset at us. She allowed us to enjoy that afternoon. I'm sure she appreciated the help with the peaches, and this was our reward. Work became play and the results were clean floors. Oh, what a wonderful memory of that week and that day!

It is me again, Lord, thanking you for wonderful adults in our lives who let us work and play without criticism.

A little Georgia wisdom: Look for fun opportunities in your work. It makes the outcome sweeter.

BASEBALL KISSES

B arry and I enjoy visits with our North Carolina
grandchildren. One summer we watched the season
opener of the Blue Dogs T-Ball Team. (An interesting
name the team gave themselves; however, when their uni-

forms came, they were blue, but the name "White Sox" is printed on them. Since none of them can read, they have no idea that the words are not "Blue Dogs.") Back to the game. It was our twins Will and Julia's first game of the season. Julia was first up to bat. They started in numerical order and she is #2 (She picked the number "2" because she was the second one born.). Will picked number "5" because that is how old he is now. So, the game started with the players batting in numerical order. Julia was up to bat. She hit the ball and ran for first base! She had reminded me earlier that I was supposed to cheer for her. Of course, what she didn't know was that this proud Nanny was going to do that anyway. There is a feeling of pride when you see your baseball player at bat.

When it was Will's turn to bat, he was excited. His coach told him that he was "hot dogging" it and that if he continued, he would miss the ball. Will was showing all the confidence in the world, and I'm sure he envisioned himself as a great batter ready to "let the meat hit the ball." After several misses, Will decided to quit "hot dogging" and "let the meat hit the ball." The ball went straight toward the pitcher's mound and Will ran to first.

The game was a tough one with the opposing team showing the same aptitude as the Blue Dogs. Each took his or her turn to bat and had the opportunity to run to first base. Sometimes the player would forget he or she was the person on base and would run out after the ball when the next batter hit it. This was a learning experience for each team, their parents. and grandparents in the stands.

Each player of both teams had the opportunity to bat. When it came Julia's second time around, she approached the home base with confidence. Will yelled encouraging words to her as she stepped up to the plate. She put the bat on her shoulder, then turned toward Will and blew him a kiss.

Maybe the major league players should adopt blowing kisses as a way to encourage each other. Oh, well, it was just an idea. I guess it works better for a five-year old than it would in the major league.

Will loves to catch the ball. Well none of them really catch it, they all run after it—at the same time—and this can prove to be a real head banger. They each take it in stride and go back to their places on the field. The coach has taught them how to bend their knees and hold their gloves like real baseball players do when they are ready to catch the ball. Picture these miniature players in their cool uniforms, baseball caps, bent down with their ball mitt in their tiny hands just waiting for the crack of the bat as the ball takes off the T-stand. They are looking at their parents for approval and sometimes must be reminded to keep their eye on the ball.

We have the second game on Thursday. It will be another interesting game being played for four and five-year old's. Julia gladly let a teammate have her turn on first base when he cried at the first game. She told him she would take the next turn. Will is working on not getting angry at himself when he misses the ball and another teammate gets to it first. The team is a work in progress.

What do adults learn from watching a T-ball game? We learn that it doesn't matter whose turn it is to bat; I can wait for mine. We learn that if a friend is on the other team, we cheer him on too. We learn that it is just a game, and it no matter who wins, it was fun to play.

It is me again, Lord, thanking you for the opportunity to watch a T-ball game where children come with no expectations of doing anything more than having fun with another group of children.

A little Georgia Wisdom: Enjoy life's lessons from a child's point of view. It looks a lot different from their perspective.

BATHROOM
SWEETS

My cousins in crime were reminding me that I didn't finish the "Sweet Potato" story. They insisted that the rest of our mischief must be revealed in order to make adults aware of the dangers of the shenanigans of children. So, folks, sit back and listen and, by all means, learn. If nothing else, you will never look at chocolate and peppermint chewing gum in the same way again.

In the middle 1950s, one could buy a pound of coffee in tin cans with a neat little key that opened the lid. The cans and lids were used by us as cooking utensils in homemade playhouses, but that is another story for another day. The adults saved them and used the cans for storing small items. Lucky for us, Aunt Gladys and Uncle Tim were coffee drinkers and had several saved for future use. Those one-pound coffee cans came in handy for Richard, Susan, Lynn, Glenn, and me. Dwayne was still in diapers and didn't need one.

Tom was the eldest of us kids and knew there were small packages of chocolate and chewing gum in the bathroom. So being the sweet and sharing cousins we were, we split the packs so every one of us had either chocolate squares or tiny chewing gum pillows. The chewing gum tasted like peppermint. Tom helped the younger ones to divide our treasures. It was like striking gold in the bathroom. I will add here that Tom couldn't have been more than nine years old and was so generous that he shared his findings with the rest of us.

We enjoyed our goodies and played in a newly painted bedroom. Soon we all needed to use the bathroom at the same time. It was as if a stomach bug had attacked all of us at the very same time. Aunt Gladys thought quickly and started passing out the small empty coffee cans. All of the younger children had one, while Tommy got the commode. It was a busy and smelly time.

If memory serves me correctly, the chocolate and gum wrappers cleared up the mystery of the stomach virus. Tommy had found chocolate Ex-lax and Feen-A-Mint gum laxatives. Fortunately, we were sweet children and shared our treasures, which kept us from overdosing. We also had a bottle of children's aspirin and shared the tiny orange-tasting treats. The Lord took care of us. There were enough children that when we shared, we prevented a fatal outcome.

It is me again, Lord, thanking You for watching over small children who love to plunder.

A little Georgia wisdom: Children love to explore. They *will* find your stash of *goodies*.

BITTERSWEET MEMORIES

One of the earliest memories of my grandparents was one Christmas in 1951, when my parents and I stayed at their house on Christmas Eve. I was three years old and was just learning about Santa Claus. It was a Christmas Eve in Georgia, so there was no snow for the reindeer to leave tracks on the roof; however, there was still proof that Santa had been inside the house. On Christmas morning, there was a footprint in the ashes of the fireplace; I knew that footprint was evidence Santa Claus had brought the tricycle that sat under the tree to me.

Over the years, as our family grew, each Christmas, we would gather at Granny's and Granddaddy's house with wrapped gifts for the tree. We celebrated birthdays at their house and Sunday dinners. Sunday dinners consisted of fried chicken and home-canned green beans, hot biscuits, gravy, banana pudding, and cake. Mama made the chocolate cake. As I tell you about these gatherings and meals, I can feel the atmosphere of family. We were strong on laughter. My cousins and I enjoyed each other's company, which included expanding families with new husbands, new wives, new babies, and new lives.

The first Christmas after my grandfather passed away, my grandmother couldn't bear to celebrate. My cousins Debbie and Renee, along with my sister Sherry, went to her house to talk her into Christmas. Those young ladies were very persuasive! We had Christmas at Granny's! However, the atmosphere hung thick with the emptiness of not having Granddaddy sitting in the rocker, smiling at all his family, but we all agreed we were so happy to have our tradition of Christmas. This tradition carried forward until my grandmother was diagnosed with cancer. She passed away January 1, 1994, at the age of eighty-four. My grandfather died at the age of sixty-seven. This seems young now that I am only three short years away from being sixty-seven years old.

My memories of the years between 1948 and 1994 always include Granny and Granddaddy. They worked hard. My grandmother would set the alarm clock fifteen minutes fast so my granddaddy would not be late for work at Schnadig (International Furniture Company). He worked there until retirement. Sure, he knew the clock was fast, but I think it was a game he played with Granny. She would have breakfast ready, and he would eat, and he didn't seem to be in a hurry to leave the house for work, and all the while, Granny would be saying, "Ed, you're gonna be late." I don't think he ever was.

Granny loved flowers and her garden. She and my aunt Mildred would plant, hoe, gather, and can the bounty from that garden. After Granny died, she left behind boxes of canned green beans. The Jolly Green Giant would have been proud!

Once, we all went camping in Panama City, Florida. Granddaddy decided he wanted a pair of shorts to stay cool. Granny wouldn't wear them then. Years later, on another trip to Florida, she decided she would get her a pair and wear it. She liked her Florida shorts (Granddaddy would have enjoyed her adventurous side). She would not wear them at home in Northeast Georgia but always when she traveled to the beach. I hope I can find their pictures to share with you all. Granny might not like it, but I think she would eventually find the humor in sharing them. Granddaddy wouldn't care. He would just smile that crooked smile.

Granny taught me how to plant tomato plants and make turkey dressing for Thanksgiving. Mama taught me the art of canning green beans, but I still don't like to do it, so I will admit we don't have home-canned green beans at our home.

Growing up with family surrounding you is special. We farmed back in the 1950s. I sound like I was a hard worker. I guess since Granny made me a small cotton pick sack to sling on my shoulder when all the women worked one cotton season picking cotton that I qualify as a farmer. I hope you saw my picture on the tractor with my granddaddy. Does that make me a farmer? I would like to think so; however, I didn't like to work in the garden. *That* was hard work.

I did my fair share of what we called stringing beans. Some people would call this snapping beans. We always had to make sure we had the ends off to pull the string from the beans before we broke them into smaller pieces. Each person had newspaper spread in his or her lap for the beans that were to be de-stringed. (Is that a word?) Then we left the strings and ends in our laps and threw our broken beans into a common metal dishpan for washing and, later, cooking. So many families came to help that there were so many of us working together on summer evenings, and we had to have several pans so we could sit in a circle under the shade tree and still reach a pan. Now as I tell you about it, it sounds fun. The talking and fellowship was fun; the work was not. It was work.

If you have followed my blog, you can guess that within this short story are many insights into life just waiting to be shared. In those years, between 1948 and 1994, there were many, many lessons that I was fortunate to learn at the feet of some extraordinary folks. This is just the beginning. The old rooster story and the attack on this *farmer* is for another day.

Sometimes I think I would love to go back for a day and relive that time, but I would have to go through the heartache of losing our loved ones again. No, like the song says, "I couldn't live there anymore."

It is me, again, Lord, thanking You for the bittersweet memories that shape the person I am today.

A little Georgia wisdom: Savor even the small moments in life. It is those moments that add the flavor to your character.

BLESSED BE THE TIE THAT BINDS, EVEN IN GRIEF

I have written about Mama and Daddy too. There is so much more to say about my parents. I have been so angry at them for dying. It has been fourteen years since Mama passed away on April 19, 2006. Those years have taken our whole family on a journey one prays no other person has to take; however, we all must face the death of a loved one. Some folks face it gracefully; they appear to grieve and move forward. Some refuse to accept it and can't emotionally move on, while others get angry.

First, let me say I know about the five stages of grief: (1) denial, (2) anger, (3) bargaining, (4) depression, and finally, (5) acceptance. I don't remember the denial stage when Mama died. She had been sick for such a long time. Sometimes, during her illness, I felt angry because she was sick. I prayed for her. I encouraged her to be strong, but it was as though the mother I knew growing up was not the mother whose frail body was not getting well. It was as if she refused to get better. My mama had always been a strong woman, and to see her frail was heartbreaking.

The bargaining stage came early on in Mama's illness. "Please, God, make her well. I know I have not been the perfect daughter, but I will be." "Please, God, let her get better. We will all help her take better care of herself." "Please, God, make her comfortable. Please don't let her suffer." I'm sure my siblings were praying these same prayers for her.

As time passed and Mama's improvements were in waves, we felt encouraged for short periods of time. When the doctor gave her only forty-eight hours, she rallied back. Thank you, Jesus. Prayers were answered! God gave her more time!

She fell and broke her hip. She almost died again, and, again, we all prayed. God answered. She was improving. Mama was given another opportunity. We were so thankful.

After each time, she was more tired, and finally, she didn't have the strength to keep going. Blood clots formed and then moved. I think Mama felt it was time to go, and her prayers for God to take her were answered. It is easy to overlook the fact that while we were praying for Mama, she may have had a prayer request of her own.

There have been years of depression watching Mama endure the pain of her illness. COPD is painful, and she often felt as if she were drowning. She was on oxygen 24-7 and feared that she might run out when she had to go on a portable to go to the doctor or, when she was able, on a shopping trip.

I don't know if I have truly accepted my mother's death. I think about her every day, and each day is easier than the day before, but I still have the pain of not being able to ask her to clarify situations or ask her for her advice. I am not sure that I am over the anger of her leaving too soon, but that was not my choice. God controls every aspect of our lives, and I am sure He was calling her to come home. I would not be human if I didn't feel the anger, but I do realize that God is in control, and He knew her pain.

Our family will never be the same now that our mother and dad have passed away. How do you heal that pain? Each of us grieves in our own way. Each of us has gotten to our own personal stage of the grief process, and how we handle that stage and transition to the next step in the grieving process is up to the individual person. God will help us mend the heartbreak each feels; however, what we need to realize is that each one of us is grieving.

It is me again, Lord, thanking You for Your grace to sustain us through the grieving process.

A little Georgia wisdom: Remember that no matter how many members are in a family, each has to deal with grief in his or her own way. We should never judge another person's grief or underestimate the grief process.

MY "BROTHER" RAY

P eople come into our lives many ways. We are connected by chance, by choice, and by birth. It is by birth that I met my "brother" Ray.

Ray is six years and three days older than I. He probably waited anxiously for his older sister to bring home a new baby and make him an uncle. I guess I was his birthday present. For years, we shared birthday celebrations and birthday cake. Once, I complained, and they baked two cakes. Ray never seemed to mind how we celebrated our birthdays, and as we grew up, he didn't mind having his younger *sister* to tag along.

Ray taught me how to ride a bicycle, to swim, to dance, and to sing. (He was an excellent pianist and organized a group of us young teens to sing specials in church.) He also told me about Santa Claus, including the details about how he had helped wrap the presents. That little bit of information about Santa could have waited for a couple of more years.

In the summer, we spent many days at Russell Lake with friends and cousins. I was always with him. I loved the idea he could drive and didn't mind having me tag along.

Once, my cousin Susan and I rode to town with him in his 1954 Ford. Susan and I waited in the hot car with the windows down while Ray ran into the post office. A nice newer model car pulled up beside us. There was a young girl, much like ourselves, sitting with the windows up. We knew she had air-conditioning in her new car. Not to be outdone by our parking space neighbor, Susan and I rolled up our windows. We sat there with sweat rolling down our faces to the point we could barely breathe. Wait, you are getting ahead of me.

Ray came out of the post office. He opened the door and asked if we were crazy. Several factors came into play: (1) the car was not running; therefore, the air conditioner could not run, and (2) Ray's 1954 Ford did *not* have air-conditioning.

Susan and I were sitting in a hot car in a ninety-degree weather with the windows rolled up. It took a long time to live this little episode down, and he told everyone about our adventure with (out) air-conditioning.

I have so many wonderful memories of my time with Ray. He carried me to church. He helped me with homework when I didn't want to do it. He encouraged me in my pursuit of a higher education. He listened to my pain when I needed an ear, and he offered gentle advice when I needed it the most.

The day he married, I was maid of honor, and Margaret's brother was best man. I cried after the wedding when no one could see. I felt I had lost him forever; however, he never let that happen.

Ray was drafted in the army, and while he was in Officer Training School in Columbus, I rode a bus to stay with Margaret for a weekend. I was his sister. When his daughter was born, I felt I was an aunt. It was a wonderful experience having an older *brother*.

Years later, when Barry and I got married, Ray escorted me down the aisle. We had come full circle.

I have so many heartfelt and funny stories about growing up in our little part of the world. I think, like many younger siblings, I embarrassed him many times, but he never stopped loving me, nor me him. As I continue to write, I will share more stories about my *brother* Ray.

There was the time when Susan and I went cruising with her brother Tom and Ray. That day, they got so mad at us for flirting with boys and drove us back home. It wasn't the flirting that made them so angry; it was the fact the boys started following us in their car. (We continued to encourage them by waving from the back seat.)

When Ray and Tom got out of the car, they were so mad they took a shortcut and jumped a bush to tell on us. My mom said later that she knew by the way they jumped the bush, they were mad at something we had done. That anger didn't last any longer than it took for them to tell on us. We loved them for that short-lived temper.

God brings people we need into our lives, and they teach us lessons. Some lessons are just too hard, and we long to forget them; however, some folks are God's gift to us. Ray was my gift.

It is me again, Lord, thanking You for the people who enter our lives by chance, by choice, and especially by birth.

A little Georgia wisdom: Never forget those who are responsible for caring, loving, and shaping the person you become.

TEACHERS COME IN SPECIAL PACKAGES

January 15, 2011, was a special day. My grandson Cameron was eighteen years old. This is the age when young men sign up for Selective Service or the draft for the military even though one has not been implemented since 1973. It is time for young men and women to register to vote. Eighteen years of age is a turning point in a teenager's life.

Cameron is a special young man. God has given him to us for a reason: to teach us. Cameron teaches us unconditional love. He doesn't speak, but he communicates his love to all of us with his gentle manner and loving ways and his sweet smile and the feel-it-all-over laughter.

Cameron teaches us that we don't need words to tell others how we feel, and he teaches us that music is a universal language; the rhythm is the same. Cameron reminds us of this when he follows the rhythm of his favorite country music songs with his toy tambourine. A regular-size tambourine is too heavy for his little frail arm to hold for very long. His small tambourine goes everywhere with him.

Cameron needs special care. He depends on others to take care of his needs, and in return, he gives love and understanding. Cameron does not judge people. He accepts them. We have learned these life lessons from him.

Cameron will never be able to drive a car or play baseball. He will never run the Peachtree in Atlanta on July 4, but he will continue to win our hearts over and over again as he melts us with his sweet smiles and his feel-it-all-over laughter. No, he will not register to vote in the 2012 elections. He won't even care who the candidates will be on the ballots. He might, however, be affected by Obamacare as a low-priority medical care patient. I am not sure where he would fit on that scale. I shudder to think about it.

Cameron turned eighteen years old. We were not sure how long we would have him with us when he was first born and weighed one pound and thirteen and a half ounces. The doctors could not assure us that Cameron would reach this age, but the Lord has blessed us with Cameron, who will forever be our *little* man.

It is me again, Lord, thanking You for a special grandson, who teaches us life lessons.

A little Georgia wisdom to grow by: Never overlook the life lessons taught from the most unusual sources. God uses all His children, even the ones with physical and mental limitations; they are the ones with the most to give.

Note: On January 15, 2020, Cameron celebrated his twenty-seventh birthday. We are so thankful for Mr. Cameron.

BRUCE AND ME

Camping in Broomstraw

Just by the title, you are ahead of me, aren't you? My cousin Bruce and I loved the outdoors. We loved to roam the fields around the house and play in the red Georgia clay. You can imagine what we looked like at the end of the day. My brother Dwayne and his brother Earl were right there with us playing; however, when this story took place, both of them were too young to be involved.

Bruce and I had huge imaginations. Everything had multiple personalities and uses. The old silver propane gas tank in the backyard was a horse we rode on trail rides or across country in a wagon train—it was an elephant the time we went on a safari across Africa. The maypops that grew in the yards and fields could be crafted into various cars, wagons, baskets, and bowls. They were sometimes used as food items when we cooked on the stove made from bricks and small board placed across them with the tin lids from Chase & Sanborn Coffee cans (these cans were useful when we all shared our chocolate *candy* and peppermint chewing gum) nailed for stove eyes.

One day, he and I decided to go camping. It is at this point that I should tell you this was out in the country. We didn't have to worry about strange people being around every corner. If someone had stopped to pick us up, we were so covered with red dirt that they would not have allowed us a ride in the car.

I still remember Mama scrubbing our clothes in a wash-tub and wringer washing machine. She had to really scrub my panties to get the dirt out. I probably had red dirt stains on everything I owned as a child.

The day Bruce and I decided to camp was a hot summer day. His mother, my aunt Opal, was at work. Mama was taking care of Earl, Dwayne, and my baby brother Eddie. I don't remember where Bruce's sister Barbara was that day, but she was not with us. Bruce and I had no supervision. Of course, up to this point, we didn't need any.

How do you light a wood stove? Every home had a box of wooden matches near the stove. We got a few to take with us from his house and began our camping journey.

Behind his house was a field of broomstraw. We played in it all the time, and it just seemed like the place to camp. We cleared us a spot to set up our camp. We didn't need much room. All we needed was a place for the two of us to sit and build our campfire.

We carefully built our fire from the broomstraw we pulled up for our campsite. Bruce lit the fire. I was afraid of the fire on the end of the match. Now, I am not blaming him for starting the fire; I am just letting you know the reason I didn't. I am just a guilty as Bruce. Remember, we were in this together.

As the fire caught, it began to spread to the surrounding broomstraw. The smoke rose above the field, and we were taking broomstraw to try to beat out the fire we had started.

The smoke rose, and we made a vow to not tell anyone about our misfortune. The more we tried to stop the fire, the more it got out of hand and spread.

To this day, I do not remember who helped us put it out, but someone helped save that whole field of broomstraw. Bruce may remember the details; I remember the fire. It was by the grace of God that the fire went away from Bruce's house. I'm sure we were punished.

It is me again, Lord, thanking You again for saving two well-meaning children from a fire.

A little Georgia wisdom: make sure you teach your children to stay away from matches and tell them to never try to put out a fire by themselves.

SILVER BELLS, SILVER BELLS

It's Christmastime in the City

It is that time of year when we rush around trying to buy the perfect gift for that special someone. In our rushing, we become irritated, tired, and just plain mean. Yes, I said mean.

People push and bump each other trying to fill their shopping carts with decorations and presents. Babies cry because they are tired and hungry. Mama is trying to get home where she will cook, clean up, decorate, and wrap presents.

Wait! It is Christmas! It is a joyous time of the year. Where is our Christmas spirit? Surely, we didn't leave it at the store.

Christmas stories on the television show beautifully decorated houses, plenty of goodies that Mama had time to make and still get her shopping completed. The snow is falling outside, and a warm, inviting fire burns in the fireplace. Awww. We want the perfect Christmas; however, our lives are not Christmas stories. They are real lives, where we get very tired; and sometimes, we lose our Christmas spirit!

If you have lost your Christmas spirit, just listen to a child. Gracie just told me, "That it was CHRIST-mas. That's the way I learned it." Out of the mouths of babes.

Children can bring us back to the reality of what we are celebrating—Jesus's birthday.

Thank you, Gracie, for reminding me that we are preparing to celebrate the birth of Jesus. This isn't about the decorations or the presents; it is about the Christ child born in a manger in Bethlehem.

It is me again, Lord, thanking You for Your birth, Your death, and Your resurrection.

A little Georgia wisdom: If you are having a difficult time getting your decorations, your shopping, your Christmas planning together, just stop and remember the real reason we celebrate Christmas.

COME IN AND MAKE YOURSELF AT HOME

"Come in and make yourself at home" was the invitation Daddy always used when folks came to visit our family on Demorest-Mount Airy Highway. Daddy and Mama wanted people to feel welcomed.

When we were younger and our friends came to visit, they became members of our family. The unspoken motto was: "if you put your feet under our table, you became family."

Mama always had the coffeepot on the stove, and the back door was always open. They loved company, but most of all, they loved family company. We have so many good memories of our aunts and uncle, cousins, grandparents, and neighbors coming to our house. Before Mama got sick, one could always have a piece of chocolate cake with that cup of coffee. Mama loved chocolate! (I will tell you one day of growing us with homemade cocoa syrup.)

When folks started to leave our home after an evening of conversation, Daddy would always say, "If any of you'ns get sick, let us know." Those were parting words that Daddy really meant.

We grew up with family around us. We got to know our family and friends as members of our own family. One never knew who might stop by, but they were always welcome. It was fun to hear the stories of times gone by or listen to the events of the day or week. We loved having that connection to folks. The kitchen table was the gathering place for the adults while we children played outside, if the weather permitted.

Making a living was hard for my parents when I was growing up, but living life was a treasure that is still buried in my heart.

There is not a day that goes by that I don't think about Daddy and Mama and the memories they left behind.

It is me again, Lord, thanking You for the memories my parents made for me and the legacy of "come on in, and make yourself at home."

A little Georgia wisdom: Friends and family come into your life for a reason. Don't miss the opportunity to love every minute of their visit.

DADDY

I have written about my daddy before, but he was such an unusual man that one writing cannot contain the love I had, and still have, for him.

Daddy had a saying for just about everything. Folks would stop by, and if he had not been feeling well, he was under the weather (sick) or he was fair to middling (feeling fine but not great)—this was also a term used for a certain grade of cotton.

One day, I asked Daddy if he was hungry. "Yes, my stomach thinks my throat's been cut."

I found myself using old sayings and idioms in the classroom. My Hispanic students probably did not have a clue to what I was saying. I have been trying to break this habit of mine, but it is a hard one to break. I grew up with Daddy.

One day, about a year before my daddy passed away, he and I were sitting in the car, waiting for my brother and sister to come out of a furniture store. Two very large ladies came out. Daddy, in a soft and thoughtful voice, said, "If those two ladies are told to haul butt, they are already loaded." Yes, that was my dad.

I miss that man. Lord knows he was hard to get along with sometimes. We had our share of disagreements, but I sure did love him. Growing up, it seemed like I felt closer to my mom. But the year after Mama died, Daddy and I got closer. I wanted Daddy to be there when I retired so we could go places together. But God had other plans for him.

Daddy missed my mama. He missed Uncle Buford. He missed Uncle Tim. All three passed away within a few months of each other. In November, the year before these three died, his brother, my uncle Clyde, died. Those deaths, so close together, really touched Daddy.

When we pray for healing for our loved ones and they don't get better like we want, one must remember this: the person we are praying to get better may be praying for God to take them home.

It is me again, Lord, thanking You for the wonderful memories of my dad.

A little Georgia wisdom: Don't get angry with God when a loved one passes and you feel your prayers weren't answered. God may have answered your loved one's prayers instead.

DADDY'S LEGACY

D addy was born on April 1, 1927. He was a year old when his mother passed away and wasn't even born when his daddy died. The picture you see of his mother was made shortly before she died of cancer. Daddy was raised by his dedicated brothers and sisters. His oldest brother, Hollis, stood firm when relatives wanted to put the younger children in an orphanage.

Uncle Hollis Smith was eighteen years old when he made a promise to a dying father to keep the family together. He kept his promise, and my dad and his siblings grew up knowing each other and continued to stay in contact with each other until they died. A closer family would be difficult to find. Uncle Clarence, Aunt Emma, Aunt Zadie, and Aunt Fannie were also very instrumental in making sure the younger children would grow up to know their family ties. Daddy was always grateful for the love of his siblings.

When their mother died, Daddy's brother, Uncle Clyde, was in the fourth grade. He carried Daddy to school with him every day. No disposable diapers, just the diaper Daddy wore that morning. The teacher would cry because she was so touched by the devotion of these children to each other. She would share her lunch with them.

Daddy was given many opportunities by folks he met along the way. He never forgot these important influences in his life. At fourteen, Daddy was taught how to drive a truck and given a job by Broughten Arial. The Arials gave Daddy a home while he was working for them. They opened their home and family to Daddy. That family meant a lot to Daddy, and on his eightieth birthday celebration, their son came to help him celebrate.

Daddy taught the five of us children work ethics. He always encouraged us to do our best work. "You are being paid for your time and the quality of work you do. Give your employer your best." Daddy believed it, and he led by example.

When Daddy went home to be with the Lord on October 2, 2007, many of the men and women who had worked for Daddy at the local furniture factory told us he was one of the best bosses they had ever had because he was fair and treated each with respect.

Before Daddy died, he had a golf cart and would travel all over the community while we were at work. We didn't know how much until he passed away. Several neighbors told us that he would ride to their houses and take the children on rides around the yard. They loved *Mr. Billy*.

Daddy never called me Sugar Bug like he called my cousins. Daddy did tell me I cooked salmon patties, gravy, and biscuits like my mama.

He would call me at six o'clock every morning and tell me it was time to get up. Barry and I would get ready for work, and Daddy would "leave the light on" for us. We cooked breakfast for him every morning. I loved that time with Daddy even though we were having to leave to go to work.

There are so many good memories of Daddy. My brother Eddie gave a eulogy for Daddy. He captured the very essence of Daddy's life and personality. Daddy didn't meet strangers and could talk to anyone who would listen. In many ways, he left that part of himself with each one of us children. One of the best memories of Daddy and me is that we were baptized on the same day together. He led by example.

There are so many things to share about both my mom and dad that it is impossible to write it all in one sitting.

It is me again, Lord, thanking You for a loving dad and for uncles and aunts who took care of him as a child.

A little Georgia wisdom: God commanded us to love one another.

DREAMING ABOUT MAMA

The weather is more like spring than winter. The little jonquil and daffodil blooms have already opened here in the North Georgia Mountains. This makes me feel like spring has arrived. Spring makes me miss Mama even more. It was in spring that she went home to be with our Lord Jesus Christ.

I dream about Mama. I have been dreaming about her on a regular basis since she died. I want to sit and talk to her. In my dreams, the coffeepot is either brewing or we are just putting on the pot. She is not sick in my dreams. But the sad part of my dream is that she and I don't sit down and talk. Isn't that strange? One would think that I would be sitting with her, drinking coffee, laughing and talking.

Maybe my dreams are really trying to tell me something. Mama and I had unfinished business together.

Mama was a major reason I was able to earn my degree from Piedmont College. I knew that my two children were cared for each day. I could relax in classes knowing that I did not have to worry about their well-being.

If your parents are still with you, clear the air of unfinished business before they are gone. I always wanted my mama to be proud of me and my accomplishments, but I don't think she was. I made mistakes in my personal life that haunted my relationship with my mom.

The Lord has forgiven me, but I have a hard time forgiving myself. Do you ever feel that way? It is harder to forgive one's self than to forgive others.

One year, for my birthday, I sent Mama a dozen roses to say thank you for giving birth to me. There are so many other things I wished I had done for her. I should have told her more just how much she meant to me.

It is me again, Lord, thanking You for forgiveness even when I can't forgive myself.

A little Georgia wisdom: Make sure you tell your loved ones how you feel. It's good for the soul.

EVERY DAY'S
A PICNIC

G rowing up in the fifties was an adventure. My cousins Bruce and Earl lived across the dirt road from us.
Bruce and I spent many hours roaming the pastures,
woods, and fields. We walked barefoot and didn't seem to
notice the rocks, hot red Georgia clay, and thorns. Strange

that today, a trip across the grassy yard without shoes is a major ordeal.

Near Bruce's house was a deep ditch. We loved that ditch. Many days were spent sliding down the banks of the ditch, walking on a board bridge across the ditch, and hiding from attacking forces in the ditch. This ditch was a fortress that could not be penetrated. We were a strong force against evil! Covered with the red dust from the ditch, we would find other adventures to keep two children occupied for the rest of a hot summer day. These adventures would last well into the evening, when the lightening bugs made their appearance and taunted us to catch them. Mason jar in hand, we filled our tiny world with light and then released them to catch another night.

Lunch was always the main meal of the day. We referred to lunch as dinner; the evening meal was supper. Mama would have fresh vegetables from the garden, fried potatoes, cornbread, and tea. Bruce and I would make our plates and carry our food outside to eat. We had a picnic every day! We just didn't realize how lucky we were growing up in small community of relatives where there were no fears and small children roamed freely to explore God's world as only children can see it. Our imaginations had no limits.

The silver propane gas tank in the backyard was sometimes the elephant we rode across Africa on a safari looking for lions. On another day, it was our faithful horse that carried us across America with a wagon train. We were pioneers fighting our way across the plains and Rocky Mountains to settle in California. With an imagination, one can do and be anything. We made sure that our world was an adventure on those hot Georgia days of summer in the fifties.

We created houses from anything we could find. Two rocks and a piece of wood would become a seat or a stove or the inside of a covered wagon. Whatever we needed to make our imaginations come to life, we created. We didn't ask anyone to help us; we were just visionaries in our own right. We were storytellers, and when all the cousins were together, we would conjure up a scary story to make Alfred Hitchcock proud. I was never the good scary storyteller, but Cousin Tom was. He would have us looking over our shoulders in the dark. The late evening shadows took on new meaning when Tom told a story.

We didn't know it at the time, but those long summer days in the North Georgia Mountains would shape the very being of who we are today. It helped shape the directions our lives would travel into adulthood. It shaped our lives into compassionate people. We knew how to play together and work together. It taught us teamwork was the best work.

The years have separated us. We don't visit anymore because our families are growing. Once a year, because of my aunt Zadie, we have a family reunion. We gather and reminisce, but it is not the same as it was when we had our plates balanced on our laps outside under the shade trees in my parents' backyard, where we had a picnic every day. We are adults now. Adulthood brings a different viewpoint of life. The innocence of children who played and worked together to bring imagination to life is gone. Our focus is on our families and on our children, who will never know the creativity of hot summer days in the North Georgia Mountains. They will never know of the night games we played in the shadows of the evening, where the stars were so visible one wanted to reach out and pick one. Our children will never have the fun of being free to roam the fields, woods, and pastures of long ago. They will never know how that freedom feels. They will never taste the coldness of the water drawn from a deep well in the backyard. The water was so cold it hurt our teeth, but it tasted oh so good! Our children will never know the fun of playing baseball in the pasture on a Sunday afternoon. Back in the 1950s, every day was a picnic.

It's me again Lord, thanking You for childhood friends who made growing up an adventure.

Just a little Georgia wisdom reminding you to call up a childhood friend and reminisce about old times.

FALL'S A COMIN'

Don't you just love this time of year? The cooler weather is beginning to make its journey into our mountain foothills. The mornings whisper with a cooler breath. You know what I mean, the coffee-drinking-on-the-porch weather. I just love fall.

There is just something refreshing about stepping out in the morning chill and seeing your breath. "Brr," we say as if we are complaining, but we are excited. Excited because winter is not far away.

Did anyone count the number of foggy mornings we had in August? The old folks say that's how many snows we will have this winter. I forgot to count from the beginning, so I guess it will be a surprise to me when the snow comes.

This fall, we are having family over to gather outside for a barbecue. My hope is that the weather is chilly enough to be refreshing yet warm enough and pretty enough to be gathered outside. I want the children to roast marshmallows this year and the campfire to feel good. Oh goodness, I can feel it already.

I love the outdoors, but I hate the bugs. When it is cooler, the bugs leave us alone, which means no itching and swatting at the uninvited guests. So maybe, just maybe, it will be a cool night, and the bugs will stay snugly curled up wherever bugs go to snuggle.

We had such a dry summer that our grass has begun to crunch. Today, it is raining, so the grass will turn green again. The leaves on our trees in the yard have already started to turn colors. Jack Frost is making his rounds with his paints, and he is decorating our trees for fall. I hope he has time to get them all done before our barbecue. Wouldn't that make for a colorful picnic?

My cousin Jack (not to be confused with Jack Frost) plays with a bluegrass band called Bluegrass Traditions. They will entertain the folks with bluegrass and gospel songs. A close friend of the family is bringing his karaoke so others can sing if they want. We have a lot of family members who play several instruments and sing. I am not one of them. I have two very young nephews under the age of ten years old who play the violin, or fiddle if it's country, and maybe they will play a tune or two.

My cousin Bruce plays guitar and sings. Bruce, don't forget that guitar! His dad, Uncle Clyde to me and the others, would come to the family reunions through the years and play and sing. Uncle Clyde was asked by the Singing Cowboy, Gene Autry, to join him in his shows, but Uncle Clyde had family commitments back home in Georgia and chose not to stay in California.

Wow, this is exciting. Out-of-town family we see only once a year, joining our local families for pictures and fun. We can sit and talk, sit and eat, sit and listen to music, eat and listen to music, and enjoy each other's company. Hey y'all, it's fall!

Fall, I am so glad you are coming. The yard is looking forward to the new colors you and Jack Frost will use for decoration. We are all looking forward to the cooler temperatures you bring with you. Fall, you are invited to sit a spell and eat barbecue and listen to gospel and bluegrass music. After all, Fall, you are a member of the family.

It is me again, Lord, thanking You for fall and family. The two go well together.

A little Georgia wisdom: Enjoy the seasons as they come. God has blessed us with the changes, so be thankful for the uniqueness of each one.

GOD USES
CUCUMBER
SANDWICHES

God uses people when they least expect it. A trip to the grocery store and the purchase of cucumbers and cream cheese became a mission field. One never knows when God will speak to you or even how He will speak to you. I certainly didn't realize that my decision to buy cucumbers and cream cheese was a message sent by God.

My best friend, Kathy, has been planning for weeks for *Tres Dias*, an interdenominational Christian weekend. Kathy is working in the dorms for an all-ladies weekend. She has been purchasing different crosses and other items to be used as focal points on her assigned table. She and I have enjoyed shopping for the various items; so indirectly, I have been involved with her mission work.

Last night, on the phone, we planned to meet for breakfast. She told me she was trying to determine how to go to her daily job and make cucumber sandwiches in time for a meeting after school. When the list of food items had made its way around the room, only the cucumber sandwiches were left on the list. How could she keep them fresh and not soggy? She would not be able to make them the day of the meeting because of time restrictions, so I volunteered to make them for her. "I can't ask you to do this!" she exclaimed.

"You didn't ask me, Kathy. I am volunteering. Let me do this for you."

You see, Kathy has been a godsend to me on many occasions. She is truly a best friend in every way. The least I can do for her is make a few sandwiches.

"Kathy, I have cucumbers and cream cheese at home to make them, and I am the only one at home who likes cucumbers. For the life of me, I don't know why I had bought so many cucumbers and cream cheese. Perhaps it was because I thought I was going to use them in my salad but I didn't. I still have the cucumbers."

This morning, Kathy and I enjoyed breakfast together. I learned God was using me to help Kathy. Isn't He an awesome God?

Kathy had been praying for God to show her a way to make this work for her. She wanted this Tres Dias to have a wonderful start, and her plans for this to go smoothly was falling apart. A coworker/friend suggested she ask the family consumer science teacher, who has a cooking class. The students enjoy doing different food requests. Their clients supply the ingredients, and the students put it together. Learning takes place! Before she could ask for their help, the family consumer science teacher told the office the students were behind in the requests for different cooking projects. Now this idea was not an option at all.

At the same time, Kathy was praying for God to show her a way to complete all her tasks. I was buying groceries. I was buying cucumbers and cream cheese! When Kathy and I realized what was taking place and how God was moving through us, we couldn't help but be in awe of how God works.

Kathy was certainly doing what God had called her to do in this mission field, and God used me to help her.

It is me again, Lord, thanking You for the testimony of a best friend who lives her life for You.

A little Georgia wisdom: no matter how small you think your contributions are, God can use you.

GRANNY DYAL'S
BOX OF SHOES

M any interesting people cross our paths and leave their marks. One such lady was Granny Dyal. Granny Dyal was not my blood relative, but neither was Aunt Mandy Broome or Aunt Bessie Stephens.

This story is about Granny Dyal and her box of shoes. Bruce shared his granny Dyal with me and this story about her prayer closet with her boxes of worn shoes.

"Granny Dyal was a true Scot through and through," he said. She knew how to feed a large family and could choke a nickel to death. Raised on a farm, there was no need to buy such things that today would cost nearly $20 a pound. She knew how to farm. What today we call free-range chickens, we could always count on a pot of dumplings or fried chicken at least once a week, and she would never miss the chicken that was taken because there was always an ample supply of chickens in the chicken yard.

Pork was easily found and in abundance from the vast swamp areas from the Altamaha River that was nearby. Men of the family would hunt the wild hogs and bring the babies home to raise in the pasture. The kids would go fishing nearly daily in the ponds that were in the pastures, so fried fish and grits were a daily staple for breakfast, and sometimes for supper too. Granny was never idle for very long. She always had things to do. Although not a very big woman, she was strong in grit and determination to manage what she had.

One could recognize her from a distance by the old-style bonnet she wore to shade her face from the hot South Georgia sun. She wore an oversized apron that draped amply below her knees with pockets on either side, one for her snuff and the other held a small sharp pocketknife. The apron wrapped nearly all the way around her waist. In her '80s, her hair was not as white as mine is now. Born in a log cabin in the late 1800s, she and my granddaddy raised a family of five children in the same log cabin where my mother and all her siblings were born. Farming a few hundred acres, they grew cotton, peanuts, tobacco, corn, and watermelons amid other crops that could be sold at the auction barn come harvest.

My granny Dyal was a marvel of a woman; she never wasted anything—not even the feathers off the chickens that she harvested. She saved the softest, most select ones and washed them and stored them between two window screens held together with a brick on top so the feathers could dry in the hot Southern sun. She mixed them with the down from geese, ducks, and turkeys, and make the softest pillows, and of course, her famous feather mattresses that we all laid on at night.

When I was a little boy and would spend summers in South Georgia, I would, at times, sleep with Granny Dyal in her feather bed. One night, at bedtime, Granny went to her closet and pulled out three boxes of shoes. Most of them were small children's shoes that were old, stiff, and worn. Many had been mended by her own hand with small thin twists of wire that had sewn together to hold the bottom of the shoe to the top of the shoe. I was worried that she would find the same need to fix my soon-to-be worn-out shoes that I was outgrowing. There were ladies' shoes with heels and men's work boots that were old and stiff and moldy, and I wondered if they were still wearable. Inquiring about them, I was told that they were once worn by my mother, her two sisters and two brothers, along with all their children and even some great-grandchildren. Granny was widowed before I was born, so these shoes represented those that she loved the most.

She lined them in rows on the foot of the bed, then she knelt and started to pray. Lovingly holding, in turn, one pair of shoes at a time, she hugged and prayed over each. She recalled who owned each pair. She picked up and held another pair that I recognized as mine that I had outgrown the year before, then she prayed over my younger brother Earl's little shoes. I was so touched and moved by that experience that I've never forgotten her prayer closet that held those boxes of old shoes.

As Bruce shared, these shoes were not the fancy go-to-church shoes she might save for Sunday but old shoes of her family, children, and grandchildren. The shoes dated all the way back to the turn of the century through about 1960. There were baby shoes worn thin by the tiny feet which outgrew them for larger ones, little girl's and boy's shoes, ladies' shoes, and men's work shoes that showed repair after repair and were finally beyond being wearable.

Granny Dyal kept the worn-out shoes with holes in the bottoms or with wire stitches that held the soles to the top of the shoes. Shoes that had walked hot fields and traveled long South Georgia tobacco rows behind an old horse or mule. Shoes that helped a young bride walk to meet her groom. Shoes that carried a future soldier to sign up for war. Granny Dyal had saved the shoes of her loved ones.

Let us remember Granny Dyal and her nightly routine of pulling that box of shoes out from the closet. One by one, taking out a pair of shoes and clutching them tenderly and prayed. "Lord, please bless and protect my daughter (etc.) and her family." Her children and grandchildren lived away, far and wide, but these old shoes kept all of them close to her, especially when she was worried when someone got sick or hurt. She would pull out that old box of shoes. What is especially important to remember was that no one knew about that old box of shoes but Granny Dyal and her grandson Bruce.

After Bruce witnessed his Granny and her prayers over those shoes, he would take the shoes and try them on. His granny scolded him, for to her, they were sacred. The life of those old shoes was gone, but she had found a new purpose for keeping them. Granny Dyal died in 1973 at the age of eighty-four, and in that box was another pair of shoes. These were from her great-grandson Michael, Bruce's son.

I asked Bruce if he would contribute this story. He was more than willing to honor the memory of Granny Dyal.

It is me again, Lord, thanking You for the love and prayers of our loved ones like Granny Dyal.

A little Georgia wisdom: The example of love shown by Granny Dyal is one we all need to remember. We need to pray for one another. Our prayers are heard by a loving heavenly Father. The faith Granny Dyal had that God was always listening is the faith God wants us to have. Prayers for others is a blessing we receive as well.

GRANNY'S LEGACY

Christmas is over. The pretty paper is in strips and shreds in plastic garbage bags and forgotten boxes. The family has been here and gone. It is over until next year.

A life's lesson is found in Christmas gifts. It is the one time when all the presents are under the tree at the same time. As we call each name one at a time, we enjoy the excitement in the eyes of the children, and then it happens—one child got a present or two more than another. It doesn't matter how much their presents cost; it is the quantity of presents under the tree that counts.

In our lifetime, we search for quantity sometimes and forget about quality. I saw this firsthand when my grandmother fought so hard with cancer. The doctor asked her if she wanted a quality life or to take treatments that would give her quantity of life. She chose quantity. Sometimes she was so sick she could barely sit up. She knew that there was no chance of recovery at her age of eighty-four and the severity of the cancer, but she decided to fight it. The harsh treatments did give her, at age eighty-four, a few more months.

Even though she suffered with sickness and pain, she got to see her first two great-great-grandchildren. I have the treasured picture of five generations together. She may have missed them had she chosen quality.

Only our Lord knows what our future holds. It is like the brightly wrapped presents under the tree; the person who gives it knows what it is and how much it is worth. It is only when it is opened that the receiver can decide what it is worth to him or her.

I am thinking about my grandmother as the anniversary of her death, January 1, approaches. She was a brave woman, who loved her children and grandchildren and fought a brave battle to stay with them as long as possible.

When we were told of her diagnosis of cancer, I prayed for God to heal my granny. I prayed and prayed for a miracle of healing. As her days passed and I saw how sick the medicine was making her and how much pain she was in, I prayed that God would lessen her pain and make her comfortable. I prayed for comfort. There came a time when the morphine was causing her to sleep more to control the harsh pain. I prayed for God's will to heal her in her heavenly home. "God, if it be your will, please release her from her earthly body to be with You and be healed. God, please show mercy."

Granny was in the hospital on morphine for the intense pain when God called her home. There was the sadness of losing her on earth but a relief to know she was not suffering anymore.

I think about her often. I think about all the good times, the laughter, the Christmas Eves spent at her house with family. I do not dwell on the cancer days. I don't like that memory. I want to remember the strong woman whose mother passed away when she was young and whose family helped her dad take care of her. I want to remember the strong woman who loved to build things, plant flowers, raise a garden, cut her own grass, and love to eat rib eye steaks and bring pieces of that steak home to her cat. I want to remember how she could not contain her excitement to have a gift that she paid my brother a quarter to tell her what was in the brightly colored package. That's what I remember about Granny—the good things that made her the person she was.

When my granddaddy passed away suddenly, she was a rock for the family to lean upon. She pulled herself together and was the strength we all looked to during this tragic time. I am sure that when she was alone, she let herself grieve for him; however, she never shared that grief with us. I believe she wanted to be the rock. She wanted to grieve in private. I saw a lot of her strength in my mother too. Mama had that same control under pressure that my granny demonstrated.

It is me again, Lord, thanking You for a wonderful legacy of a strong grandmother.

A little bit of Georgia wisdom: Enjoy the moments you do have, and search for the quality of life you want. It could be your quality of life is hidden in the quantity of life God gives you.

HOG-KILLIN' WEATHER

Reading a post on our family website written by my cousin Lynn brought back a lot of memories. I remember when it was hog-killing weather, which was usually winter when it was really cold outside. It was an all-day affair to process the hog, but everyone around would help.

I have seen Granny process sausages in Mason or Ball canning jars. She and Granddaddy had a smoke house in which they hung the salted hams. I don't remember them ever smoking the hams, but we still called it the Smoke House.

Mama used to fry the fresh pork chops in the black iron skillet. After she took up (removed) the meat, she would pour hot coffee into the grease and make red-eye gravy, which we poured over a biscuit.

Once, Daddy butchered a hog, and there was all this fresh pork. Mama had been cooking and eating this fresh meat all day and, during the night, had a gallbladder attack. She had to have major surgery. She almost died from the combination of a highly infected gallbladder and the surgery, and it was triggered from all the fresh pork.

One of my favorite meals is fried fat back, small green onions, green beans, tomatoes, cucumbers, and cornbread with fresh butter on the cornbread. Add some fried potatoes, and you have the perfect meal.

These are wonderful memories of a time when we grew and processed our own food. I would have no idea how to process the meat the way my parents and grandparents did. Good thing we have grocery stores.

The good old days really means the hardworking days. So thankful we don't have to depend on my knowledge of agriculture and food preservation; my family would've starved to death.

It is me again, Lord, thanking You for the good memories of a time long ago.

A little Georgia wisdom: when you are given opportunities to have experiences or learn from your elders, make sure you don't walk away empty-handed.

MAMA

I have been working on a story about my mama. The strange thing when writing about someone so close is that it is the most difficult piece to write. Mama taught me many things, including the love of reading. She read to me so much when I was a little girl that I memorized one of the books.

Mama would read while she churned to make butter and buttermilk. Churning is a boring job with its up and down repetitions of the churn stick in the large churn. The butter would eventually rise to the top to be scooped up and molded into round chunks of butter. The milk left after the butter was separated was the buttermilk. This took a while, and to entertain herself, Mama would read.

Mama's love for reading lead her to writing. She was a member of the Georgia Romance Writers and attended many of their conferences in Atlanta. She would share parts of her manuscripts at the conferences and wrote four complete books; however, because she was a perfectionist, she would not send them to the publishers. Harlequin requested one of her books, and an editor from another company wanted to read her work. Mama wanted it to be letter-perfect before she would let go.

Reading and writing were just two of her many hobbies. Mama was a visionary. She loved to work with her hands, and this included refinishing or making furniture. She and Granny would build furniture. They once cut a long sofa into two separate pieces to make a love seat and chair. They built bookshelves and small shelves to hold knickknacks. They were a creative duo.

Mama also loved to sew. She made our clothes when we were growing up. Years ago, when I was little, the dresses were made from flour sacks. During 1950s, one could buy flour in cloth sacks. These sacks were brightly colored, and the material was just right for making little girl's dresses. My cousins Bernice and Barbara have fond memories and more vivid memories of the flour sack dresses than I have. I wish I could remember the prints and colors of those flour sacks.

Mama was an early advocate of recycling. She used the brown paper bags from the grocery store in the kitchen. These bags were used to drain foods, such as the wonderful doughnuts she would fry. One of my favorite memories was getting off the school bus and smelling the sweet aroma of the doughnuts or cake she was making for our afternoon snack. Just thinking about it makes me long for the delicious bites of her chocolate cake. (Mama was often teased that her stove couldn't bake anything but chocolate cakes.) It took her several years to even start using paper towels. She used cloth towels in the kitchen that could be washed over and over again.

Mama loved music and could yodel (my brothers and sister don't know this tidbit of information) and took aerobics classes. She was a modern woman. Her eye for fashion was evident in her well-matched outfits. Many years after she stopped sewing, she could walk into a store, pull several items down from the rack, and the results would be a lovely suit that would be one of a kind. She knew how to combine items together to get the look she wanted. She should have gone into fashion design because she sure had an eye for it. How I wish I had inherited that trait from her!

My mama went home to be with the Lord on April 19, 2006. She had been very ill for a long time. Sometimes I get so angry at her for an early death. I wanted her to be like she was when I was a child—healthy and creative. To see someone you love succumb to illness is hard to watch. The mama I want to remember is the one listening to the radio, sewing cute dresses, and planning a trip to the beach. She would put on her bikini and get her tan in the backyard then talk my daddy into going to Daytona Beach, Florida. Daddy didn't like the beach, but he seemed to enjoy it once he was there.

I look forward to talking to Mama again. She taught us about God and the importance of being saved by accepting Jesus Christ as our personal Savior and asking forgiveness of our sins. She reminded us to read our Bibles and to pray. Every night, as each one of us crawled into bed, she would call to us a reminder, saying, "Don't forget to say your prayers." Every night, when I go to bed, I say my prayers. Mama taught us well.

It is me again, Lord, thanking You for the love of a mama who taught us to love You and the importance of talking to You.

A little Georgia wisdom: enjoy the time with your mother, read your Bible every day, and whatever you do, don't forget to say your prayers.

SWEET POTATOES ON THE WALL, WHO'S THE MESSIEST ONE OF ALL?

Children can be destructive. Those innocent little beings whose sweet smiles and affectionate adoring eyes can be deceiving. I want to try to recount an event that took place in the 1950s. An event that ended with a dirty diaper and a brand-new, just-purchased mattress being carried out of the house in a sheet. These innocent children were under the age of ten, most of them age seven or younger.

Picture a small two-bedroom house filled with family. Brothers and a sister with their spouses and their children gathered for an evening of fun. The adults are sitting in the living room, catching up on all the latest news. The children are in the bedroom playing. The youngest is in diapers, and the oldest is around nine or ten years old. We know that there were at least seven children and maybe up to nine or eleven.

We can't agree on who all was involved, but we do know the room was filled with little children. We could have started our own day care, but the adults were not supervising, or the ending of this story would have been a happy one.

We are not absolutely sure of what happened with the little ones, but it is said there was a bushel of tomatoes and a pair of suspenders involved and what looked like a little pile of creamed sweet potatoes on the wall. You are already putting this story together, aren't you?

Aunt Gladys and Uncle Tim, having moved from Florida to this cute little house on Banks Street, had just purchased a brand-new mattress for one of the beds in that small room. The children showed no mercy.

I am not going to point blame at any one of us cousins; we were all equally guilty, except the one in diapers. I'm sure he didn't know how the *sweet potatoes* got on the wall. The rest of us deserved what we got, but for the life of me, I can't remember if we were punished or if our parents were just glad to get us out of the room to clean it up. Maybe they felt the pain of guilt for not keeping a closer eye on us.

My mother told me that the room was a mess. Uncle Buford thought the yellowish orange pile on the wall was sweet potatoes, but upon examination of some on the tip of his finger and a sniff proved otherwise. The mattress had to be carried out in a sheet. (When she told this, I could just hear "Taps" being played as they carried it out of the house.) Poor mattress died before it was able to give comfort to a sleeping child.

Mama never told me the exact cause of its demise, but it was probably soaked with the tomatoes, which were propelled through the air by a pair of suspenders hooked to the bedpost. The projectiles hit the wall, and the juice from those airborne missiles slowly coated said walls as it made its way to the bed and floor.

As I wrote this story from my mother's account years ago, I called the others who were involved to get eyewitness accounts. Strangely, each remembered it in a slightly different way, and I can't remember it at all. One would think that with as much carnage that took place in that room, I would remember something; however, forgetfulness can have its own reward.

It is me again, Lord, thanking You for the love of family even when we may not deserve it.

A little Georgia wisdom: leaving children to entertain themselves may result in creative destruction!

WHO YOU CALLING OLD?

When you think of senior citizens, do you see little old ladies with their knitting in hand, rocking in a wooden rocking chair with a cushion on which to rest their aged behinds? Maybe the vision you have is little ladies with white hair and a neat and tidy bun at the nape of their necks. Can you just see the ladies knitting little caps for their grandchildren? Well, if this is what you think we ladies do, think again.

Carol and I have just started getting our social security checks. Which, by the way, we earned from all the years devoted to working for a living. We still don't feel any older than we did when we were in our twenties. Experience has taught us well, and neither of us would go back to being twenty again. We love this stage of our lives, and God has blessed us with so much love.

Cousin Carol and I, along with our cousins, grew up acting. All of my cousins, at one time or another, love to dress up and entertain. (Uncle Clyde was offered a job with Gene Autry, the Singing Cowboy, back in the day.) Carol still sings in church, and I often think back on the gifted entertainers we have had in our family, and still do. I stand amazed at the talent. Uncles and cousins who play guitar and/or piano, nephews who play violin, nieces who play guitar; and so many of them sing. Our family could start a choir and have their own band. We love music.

Carol and I like the idea of making others laugh and use silly clothes and hats—one must not forget the hats for our ensemble. Necessity was instrumental to the involvement of our granddaughters. In our debut, we were babysitting two of our granddaughters, and well, we dressed them like a mini-me and added them to our skits. They loved it, and another generation of fun-loving cousins was born.

It is the child in Carol and me who enjoys the pretending, singing, and just plain fun of what we do. Sometimes, because we have so much fun with our shows, we go over the time limits. Of course, it may be because both of us are a Smith, and we love to talk. We can talk to a fence post because the post will stand there and listen. The one subject we never tire of talking about is God's love for us. Our mission is to illustrate the love of our Lord by our enthusiasm for the gift of eternal life.

Our cast of characters has grown with my friend Kathy, and we have included more of our granddaughters. They love the results, but not the practice. We have found that as long as they are having fun with our skits and songs, they enjoy the audience. Little Julia is our youngest actress at age five years old and can be a comedian in her own right. She sits in a miniature chair behind us and makes little comments. They are her personal observations, which can be quite entertaining for us during our performance. It is probably a good thing the audience can't hear her.

Carol's three granddaughters, Hayley, Leanne, and Kaitlin, sing; and her other granddaughter Joely sings and hand signs many of our songs. My granddaughter Madison signs in American Sign Language and sings as well, and granddaughter Gracie sings too.

Our little group loves to sing the old hymns, as well as some of the newer songs. We want our granddaughters to continue their love for entertainment, but most of all, we want them to become happy Christians.

God has blessed these two *senior citizens* with a joy for living. Carol and I want to continue to grow in our Christianity with young and happy hearts. One must never get to old to enjoy talking about the love of God.

It is me again, Lord, thanking You for the precious opportunity to work with our grandchildren for Your glory.

A little Georgia wisdom: Always be open to the joys of life. Never forget what it was like to be a child, and never forget what it is like to be a child of God.

ABOUT THE AUTHOR

L inda Smith Church is a Georgia native who was born and raised in the Northeast Georgia foothills of the Blue Ridge Mountains. Growing up, her imagination took her to all the places she wanted to go.

Linda is a graduate of Piedmont College in Demorest, Georgia, where she has earned a bachelor of arts degree and an education specialist degree. She attended Brenau University and earned a master's degree in learning disabilities education. She is retired from Habersham County School Systems where she taught at the high school level. Her teaching career also included Piedmont College and Lanier Technical College in Gainesville, Georgia.

She and her husband, Barry, are parents to four adult children, thirteen grandchildren, and a great-granddaughter. Barry and Linda are both retired and living a dream job at Dollywood in Pigeon Forge, Tennessee. They are enjoying life with the people they meet each day on the park.

Linda describes herself as a baby boomer who has made it her journey through life to gather a bouquet of *lifeisms*. She says her journey has not been an easy one; the lessons were hard, but the rewards have been great. Her stories are experiences that you may have unknowingly shared with her.